DATE DUE

| | | | |
|---|---|---|---|
| | | | |
| | | | |
| | | | |
| | | | |
| | | | |
| | | | |
| | | | |
| | | | |
| | | | |
| | | | |
| | | | |

# Madeleine ALBRIGHT

Biography

Megan Howard



A&E

Lerner Publications Company
Minneapolis

***To Jedidiah—***

One person can make a difference.



Some of the people in this series have also been featured in A&E's acclaimed BIOGRAPHY series, which is available on videocassette from A&E Home Video. Call 1-800-423-1212 to order.



Lerner Publications Company
241 First Avenue North
Minneapolis, MN 55401

Website address: www.lernerbooks.com

Library of Congress Cataloging-in-Publication Data

Howard, Megan.
Madeleine Albright / by Megan Howard.
p. cm.
Includes bibliographical references and index.
ISBN 0-8225-4935-2 (alk. paper)
1. Albright, Madeleine Korbel—Juvenile literature. 2. Women cabinet officers—United States—Biography—Juvenile literature.
3. Cabinet officers—United States—Biography—Juvenile literature.
4. United Nations—Officials and employees—Biography—Juvenile literature. 5. Ambassadors—United States—Biography—Juvenile literature. I. Title.
E840.8.A37H69 1999
327.73'0092—dc21
[B] 97-27450

Manufactured in the United States of America
1 2 3 4 5 6 — JR — 04 03 02 01 00 99

# CONTENTS

*Madeleine Albright is sworn in as the first female secretary of state as President Bill Clinton looks on.*

# Introduction

On January 23, 1997, Madeleine Albright stepped to the podium in the Oval Office of the White House and faced Vice President Al Gore. With President Bill Clinton standing behind her and her three daughters—Alice, Anne, and Katherine—by her side, she placed her hand on her family Bible. As the vice president recited the oath of office, she repeated the words after him:

I, Madeleine Albright, do solemnly swear that I will support and defend the Constitution of the United States against all enemies, foreign and domestic; that I will bear true faith and allegiance to the same; that I take this obligation freely, without any mental reservation or purpose of evasion; and that I will well and faithfully discharge the duties of the office on which I am about to enter. So help me God.

With those words and a kiss on the cheek from the vice president, Madeleine Albright became the 64th U.S. secretary of state, charged with the job of working with the president and other government officials to plan foreign policy—the way the United States acts and communicates with other nations.

Although many others had held this office before Albright, this ceremony was extraordinary. For the first time in American history, a woman would head the State Department. In fact, as the top-ranking

*Madeleine Albright gets a kiss from Vice President Gore after being sworn in as secretary of state. President Clinton applauds his new appointment.*

cabinet member and a close adviser to the president on matters of international relations, she was the highest ranking woman ever to serve in the U.S. government—and she had not even been born in this country.

Although Albright has said, "Nobody ever thought that it was possible for a woman to become secretary of state," her whole life prepared her for that important assignment.

*Flanked by President Clinton,* left, *and Vice President Gore,* right, *the new secretary of state declares that "we must not shy from the mantle of leadership."*

*In a traditional Czech costume, young Madeleine,* left, *poses with her mother, sister, and brother.*

# *Chapter* **ONE**

# BRIGHT BEGINNINGS

**MARIE JANA KORBEL WAS BORN ON MAY 15,** 1937, in Prague, the capital of a country that was then called Czechoslovakia. The little girl got the name *Madlenka,* or Madeleine, from her grandmother. Madeleine's parents, Josef and Mandula Korbel, welcomed their first child into the world.

Josef Korbel, a handsome man with dark brown hair and glasses, was a rising star in the Czechoslovakian diplomatic community. The Czech government appointed him press attaché in the neighboring country of what was then Yugoslavia. Josef was responsible for communicating with Yugoslavia's journalists about matters related to Czechoslovakia. The Korbel family moved more than 500 miles from their home in

Prague to Belgrade, the capital of Yugoslavia. Josef worked in the Czechoslovakian embassy there. Although the move separated Madeleine from her grandparents and other family members for a while, she was certainly not lonely.

As the tiny girl slept in her crib, learned to crawl and walk, and played with her toys, a swirl of activity surrounded her. The doors of the Korbels' home were always open, and visitors often dropped in to discuss foreign policy and other international matters. "Belgrade was like a village in those days," a Yugoslavian friend remembers. "Everybody knew everybody else."

And everybody seemed to know Josef Korbel. Educated as a lawyer, the charming diplomat impressed Yugoslavia's diplomatic community, and many believed that he had enough skill and intelligence someday to become the prime minister, the leader of the Czech government. To Madeleine, there was nothing exceptional about the constant talk of politics and foreign relations. "We talked about international relations all the time—the way some families talk about sports or other things around the dinner table," she explained.

Although the conversation may not have been extraordinary to Madeleine, her father was. She idolized him, and while she was still very young, she decided that she wanted to be just like him. He became her first mentor, someone who guided her ideas and taught her the importance of the strength of her ideals.

Madeleine wanted her father to be proud of her. "A great deal of what I did, I did because I wanted to be like my father," she has said. Overprotective at times, Josef encouraged his family to stay close. "We all were together all the time," Albright said. "Family solidarity was what my father used to talk about."

Josef also expected to be obeyed. No punishment was worse than when he wouldn't talk to his children for a week. Hoping to avoid his wrath and displeasure, Madeleine did what many children do. She created a balance between her needs and her father's desires. For her, however, the two often merged.

*In March 1939, Hitler's Nazi troops entered the city of Brno, Czechoslovakia.*

*Chapter* **TWO**

# A FAMILY IN DANGER

**THE POLITICAL STRUGGLES THAT SHAPED MADELEINE** Korbel and her native land started before she was even born. Adolf Hitler and the Nazi party took control of Germany in 1933 and then vowed to establish a German empire in Europe. After Germany annexed (took over) Austria in the spring of 1938, Britain, Italy, and France made a treaty with Hitler to avoid war. The treaty, called the Munich Agreement, allowed Germany to occupy a Czech territory in which more than half the population was German. As a result, Germany received 38 percent of Czechoslovakia's land—which meant the end of Czechoslovakia as a viable country. The Germans forced Czech president Eduard Beneš to resign. Beneš fled to London, where he

*England's Prime Minister Neville Chamberlain,* left, *shakes hands with Adolf Hitler after signing the Munich Agreement.*

set up a provisional Czechoslovak government.

Although she was only two years old and still living in Belgrade at the time, this agreement had a lasting impact on the events of Madeleine Albright's life. On December 28, 1938, the Czechoslovakian government told the Korbels to return to Prague. Hitler soon took complete control of the country. The small Czech army could not defend itself when German troops marched into Prague.

Used to living in a democracy, the Czech people were devastated by Nazi rule. For politicians and intellectual leaders like Josef Korbel, who had served in the democratic government, life was not merely hard. It was also dangerous because the Gestapo, Germany's military police, targeted them. "Josef's name was . . . on some list of people who should be arrested," Mandula Korbel wrote in her memoirs. When German tanks rolled into Prague on March 15, 1939, Madeleine's happy, normal life ended. It was no longer safe for her to remain with her parents, who were being hunted by the Gestapo. For several days and nights she stayed with relatives while her parents roamed the streets, hiding in restaurants and shops, and spent the nights with friends who protected them.

*One Czech woman weeps as she salutes passing German troops.*

From left to right, *Foreign Minister Tituleesu of Romania, President Eduard Beneš of Czechoslovakia, and Foreign Minister Jevtic of Yugoslavia formed governments-in-exile after Hitler took power in their countries.*

Thanks to Josef's friends and government connections, the Gestapo finally granted the Korbels permission to leave the country. With two-year-old Madeleine in their arms, the Korbels said good-bye to their parents and friends and headed for the train station. "By 11:00 the same night, we all three were in a train to Belgrade with two small suitcases that we were able to pack in a hurry," Albright explained. But when the Korbels got off the train in Yugoslavia, they were not safe there either, because Yugoslavia supported the Nazis. With the help of friends, the family fled to Greece, then to Britain, where Josef's older brother, Jan, had already escaped with his family.

Dagmar Simova, one of Madeleine's cousins, came to live with the family soon after they arrived in London.

Dagmar, who was nine years older than Madeleine, often baby-sat her cousin. Dagmar had to tolerate Madeleine's bossy personality, but she found it more amusing than aggravating.

Many members of Czechoslovakia's old democratic government, including Josef, joined Beneš's government-in-exile in London. Josef headed the information department. He supervised secret radio broadcasts into his country, keeping Czechs informed about the activities of the government-in-exile. These broadcasts were crucial to those still living in Czechoslovakia, since the Nazis controlled all media and withheld all negative information about their government.

*Londoners pass the time in an underground railway station used as an air-raid shelter.*

Safe in London, Madeleine grew from a toddler to a child and began to learn English. On September 15, 1940, however, bombs shattered any sense of safety. The Germans began "the Blitz," a campaign of air raids over London. A siren blared to warn Londoners of attacking German planes, and frightened residents hurried to bomb shelters—mainly subway tunnels, backyard shelters, reinforced basements, or stairwells. The air raids sometimes lasted 10 hours, and not all shelters had bathrooms, which added to the discomfort of the close quarters. Along with everyone else, Madeleine and her family hid in an underground shelter until it was safe to emerge.

The Germans hoped to weaken civilian morale and force Britain to surrender, but with each retreat underground, London's residents learned new ways to pass the time, playing cards, singing, or talking. Madeleine remembers chasing away her fear by singing "A Hundred Green Bottles Hanging on the Wall" with her cousins.

When young Madeleine finally followed her parents out of the shelter, she inspected her adopted city. "I remember what it was like to come out of the air raid shelter and see London bombed," she recalls, although she was only three years old at the time. Former houses were now piles of bricks. Many of her neighbors' precious belongings were twisted masses of junk. As the air war continued, bombs and the threat of bombs were a fact of life for Madeleine. The air raids

*Historic St. Paul's Cathedral stands untouched amidst the rubble of London after countless German air raids.*

took place almost every night during the fall and winter of 1940.

The war had made Madeleine an extremely serious child, and she acquired an acute sense of awareness, so she might have known she wasn't completely safe anywhere during the war. Madeleine had seen the massive damage each bombing raid had caused. She remembers "thanking God for America's help," having heard from her parents that the United States was providing Great Britain with weapons and assisting with trade to England during this period.

*Two city employees,* facing the camera, *and an air-raid warden sit on top of an office building. They are on the lookout for German planes.*

The windows on all London homes were covered with heavy, dark material so no light could shine through to the outside and provide an easy target for German planes. Outside lights were also turned off at night. These measures prevented spies from sending secret light codes to the Germans. Air raid wardens checked homes to make sure everyone complied. Windows also had to be taped to prevent flying glass when the bombs hit.

Partly to escape the bombing raids, Josef and Mandula moved their small family to Walton-on-Thames, a London suburb. Still, the threat of a German bomb always hung over them. The Korbels

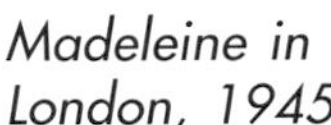

*Madeleine in London, 1945*

bought a Morrison shelter—a steel table that the makers said would protect anyone who sat under it from being killed by a bomb. "We ate on the table and we slept under the table and we played around the table," Madeleine remembers. In May 1941, Germany finally gave up its attempt to defeat Britain by air.

In December 1941, the United States entered the war as one of Great Britain's allies. In addition to the trade assistance the government was already providing, U.S. troops arrived in Europe. "When I heard that 'the Yanks were coming,' that was the first time that I fell in love with American men in uniform," Albright said.

As Madeleine began attending school, the stringent war rules continued. The British government rationed food and kept the streets dark for six long years. Life was difficult for everyone, but for Madeleine, unlike

*Nazi soldiers herd prisoners from trains into the Auschwitz concentration camp during World War II.*

her parents, the circumstances of war were the only ones she knew.

Madeleine's parents, on the other hand, held on to the hope that the war would end, and they would reclaim some of what they once had. Madeleine often escaped her own unpleasant realities by listening to her mother and father talk "about how they met, what life was like in the 1920s and 1930s in Prague and about historical figures they knew."

Mandula Korbel wrote about the war years in her memoir: "These were years of hope, and mainly, we were young." But Nazi horrors were just beginning. Hitler's troops imprisoned Jews in the countries controlled by the Nazis and shipped them to concentration camps to live—and for many, to die. In Czechoslovakia, the Germans used the concentration camp of Terezin as a holding place for Jews before they sent them to other camps, such as Auschwitz. The Korbels didn't know what was going on in their country until much later, when news of the camps reached Great Britain. Although the government-in-exile managed to get information into Czechoslovakia, tight Nazi control made it virtually impossible for information to flow the other way. While in London, the Korbels lost contact with family members who had remained in Czechoslovakia.

*Prime Minister Winston Churchill stands up in his car and gives the famous V-sign to the joyful mob celebrating the end of World War II. Some people climb a lamppost to get a better view.*

# *Chapter* **THREE**

# GOING HOME

**ON MAY 7, 1945, WINSTON CHURCHILL,** England's prime minister, announced that World War II had ended in Europe with the Nazi surrender. He proclaimed May 8—VE Day (Victory in Europe Day)—a national holiday. Church bells rang, street lights went on, and Great Britain celebrated. Cheering, dancing crowds filled the streets. For most of the country, the great news meant their homes were safe. For Madeleine Korbel and her family, it meant they could finally go back to their home.

Eight-year-old Madeleine, her sister, Katherine, who had been born in 1942, and their 17-year-old cousin Dagmar boarded a transport plane that took them home to Prague in July 1945. When Madeleine

*The house on Prague's Hradcany Square where Madeleine lived briefly before emigrating with her parents to England at the beginning of World War II*

returned home, she looked out over the city from the roof of her apartment building in Hradcany Square. She could see how well Prague had survived the long war compared to the destruction she'd seen in London. Although Madeleine had been too young to remember what Prague looked like before her family fled, she did observe that the buildings there had not been destroyed.

Still, life was not easy. Like many people returning home, the Korbels faced personal tragedy. Dagmar's parents and sister had been killed in the war, so Josef Korbel became Dagmar's official guardian, which meant that Dagmar became part of Madeleine's family. Madeleine's three grandparents had also died during the war. Her parents, however, never told her exactly how family members had died—in concentration camps. Madeleine accepted her parents' explanation that her grandparents had died in the course of the war. She never pressed her parents for more details about her family, and Dagmar still didn't have all of the information regarding the deaths. "I didn't know about the concept of the fact that they had parents," Albright explained about her lack of curiosity. "I mean, there were no grandparents when I was a little girl."

Like most of its structures, Czechoslovakia's democracy had also remained intact, thanks to the government-in-exile. In fact, the man who had lead the Czech government before the war, Eduard Beneš, became the nation's president again after the war. Because Josef had supported and worked for Beneš while in London, he was rewarded by being named ambassador to Yugoslavia. The family returned to Belgrade in September 1945, and Madeleine began her first work as a diplomat. Dressed in traditional Czech costume, she stood next to her father and greeted foreign dignitaries at the airport. She spent so much time in those days handing out flowers to visitors that she jokes, "I did it for a living."

The war had had a big impact on Yugoslavia, as it had on every other European country. During the war, the Communist Party had gained the support of the Yugoslav people. The Communists set up a temporary government in 1943, and they helped free Belgrade from German occupation in 1944. After the war, they maintained power under the leadership of Josip Broz Tito. The Korbels found themselves in a Communist country that did not welcome people who believed in democracy. Because they were afraid to associate with a diplomat who represented democratic ideals, many of the Korbels' former friends avoided the family. Josef Korbel worked closely with Yugoslavia's Communist leaders, including Tito, but his association with them was professional rather than social.

This stay in Belgrade was isolating, and Madeleine's home in the embassy was no longer the gathering spot for lively foreign policy exchanges among diplomats. But suspicion went both ways. Madeleine's parents distrusted the Communist government and kept their daughter out of school so she would not learn Communist beliefs. Instead, they hired a governess to teach her at home. When Madeleine was 10, she went to boarding school in Switzerland, where she learned to speak French, just as her mother had done when she was young.

While Madeleine was away at school, trouble began to brew in Czechoslovakia. In the 1946 election, the Communists had won control of the Czech parliament—in large part because many Czechoslovakians were grateful that the Soviet Union had rescued much of their country from the Germans. Even though the Communists had the most representatives in the parliament, however, the government remained independent, and other views were represented.

However, Josef Korbel could see that the Communists might try to seize total control of the country. If that occurred, Czechoslovakia would no longer be an independent democracy. It would become a Communist state.

In February 1948, just as Josef had feared, the Communists took over the government and banned all opposition parties. Democracy was crushed. The new government took control of farms, factories, and other businesses, and it cut off nearly all contacts with democratic countries. People were no longer allowed to travel or even communicate freely.

Because of his political beliefs, Josef and his family were not safe in Czechoslovakia under the new government. This time luck, not planning or secret hideouts, provided their escape. Czechoslovakia's deputy foreign minister offered Josef a position on a commission at the newly created United Nations (UN), an international organization that works for world peace and the betterment of humanity. Although the Communists did not want Josef to make important decisions about the politics of the country, they were happy to use his impressive diplomatic skills. And he was more than happy to use the new government for his purposes, too. Since United Nations headquarters is located in the United States, Josef saw a safe way to get his family out of Czechoslovakia by taking the UN post.

*The private school that Madeleine attended*

# *Chapter* **FOUR**

# AMERICAN GIRL

**A PROFESSIONAL TRIP TO NEW YORK CITY, WHERE** UN headquarters is located, got Josef Korbel out of Czechoslovakia, but the rest of the family had a problem. They were not government employees assigned to travel for business, so they had to think of another reason for leaving the country. If the Communist government had had any idea that they were planning to flee the country forever, they would have been severely punished. "My mother had to pretend she was taking our family from Czechoslovakia on a week's vacation," Albright explained, "when we were really leaving for good."

At the end of 1948, with only a small portion of their belongings, the Korbel family, which included

Madeleine, Katherine, their infant brother, John, and a maid, left Czechoslovakia for England. Dagmar, however, was missing from the group. Dagmar says that she was not invited to join the family in their new country, but Albright recalls that her parents told her Dagmar preferred to stay and go to school in Czechoslovakia. In either case, the Iron Curtain of Communism came down on Czechoslovakia with Madeleine and her family on one side and her teenage cousin on the other.

In his application for political asylum in the United States, Josef Korbel wrote, "I cannot, of course, return to the Communist Czechoslovakia as I would be arrested for my faithful adherence to the ideals of democracy." The United States granted his request for asylum on the grounds that the Korbels were displaced persons—people who fear they would be persecuted in their own country because of their race, ethnic background, religion, nationality, or political opinion. Madeline and the rest of her family then joined Josef in New York. When Czech government leaders learned that the Korbels would not be returning, they fired Josef and confiscated his property.

Josef had no trouble finding work since the U.S. government appointed him to work on the same UN commission. The Korbels made their new home in Great Neck, New York, where Madeleine enrolled in sixth grade at the nearby public school. At only 11 years old, Madeleine had lived in five countries and knew four languages. Because of the six years she had spent in London, she already spoke English, but she practiced talking with an American accent instead of a British one. Madeleine loved her new country, and her goal was to be American—just like the other students.

At the end of the school year, Josef Korbel accepted a teaching position at the University of Denver Graduate School of International Studies. The Ford Foundation, which grants funds primarily to educational and charitable institutions, provided money to purchase a car and find a place to live. In June 1949, the Korbels loaded themselves and what little they owned into a green Ford coupe and drove to another new home—this time in Denver, Colorado, the "Mile High City." As they headed toward Denver, the children peered out the windows of the car, waiting for it to make a steep one-mile climb into the sky, but that never happened. They hadn't realized that they'd been gradually moving to higher and higher elevations as they drove.

Because of his good fortune, Madeleine's father never let the family forget how lucky they were to have come to the United States. The daily newspaper carried the slogan, "Tis a privilege to live in Colorado." "Kids," Josef reminded his three children, "never forget that it is also a privilege to live in the United States."

While the Korbels prospered in Denver, back in Czechoslovakia, Dagmar suffered because of her relationship to Josef, a man who had embarrassed the

*At Kent, Madeleine,* third from the right in the second row, *sang in the glee club.*

Czech government. Dagmar was expelled from the university, and she had trouble getting jobs—evidence of the difficulties that the Korbels themselves might have ultimately faced if they had stayed in Czechoslovakia.

Madeleine's biggest problem was rather trivial in comparison to her cousin's woes. Madeleine had earned a scholarship to a private school, Kent School for Girls, in Denver. She and her father got into a heated argument over whether she would accept admission. Madeleine didn't want to attend a small school where she would be one of only 16 other girls in her class. Ultimately Josef won, however, and Madeleine became a Kent student. She quickly settled in at her new school and began to make a name for herself by starting an international relations club. The events of World War II and her life in a new country had strengthened her passion for foreign relations. She won a contest in eighth grade by naming every UN member state in alphabetical order. There were 51 countries in the organization at the time. "My dream was to do well, speak English well, get good grades, and start more international relations clubs, as I did at Kent," she explained about those years. In fact, Albright likes to say that one of the big perks of starting a new club each time she started at a new school was that she could appoint herself president!

A no-nonsense leader, Madeleine made the girls in the organization meet weekly to discuss foreign policy. "I'm sure some of my friends found me very boring," Albright now says about her efforts, "but that

*Madeleine started an International Club at Kent. She is sitting front center.*

*Madeleine's senior yearbook photo. Part of the entry reads, "You will often find her taking a definite stand on matters, staunchly saying, 'You guys, this just proves it!'"*

was what I was interested in, so that's what I did." She had an opinion on nearly everything and became known for her strong views, often declaring, "You guys, that just proves it!" during heated discussions with her school friends.

But Madeleine also wanted to fit into her new culture. She adopted the American nickname "Maddy" and joined the glee club as well as the chapel committee. But it wasn't always easy to be like the other girls, because of her strict, strong-willed father. When Madeleine began dating, her father insisted on going along. Although her dates were allowed to drive her to dances, her father always insisted on driving Madeleine home while the date followed in his car. To the young couple's horror, Mr. Korbel then invited the boy to come into the Korbels' home for cookies and milk. Boys didn't often ask the mortified Madeleine out again.

The excitement of life at home somehow made up for Madeleine's romantic disasters, however. She had an opportunity to learn more about international issues from people who cared about them as much as she did. Whenever her father's students dropped by the house to discuss foreign policy and international relations with him, her mother created the mood by reading palms. Madeleine eavesdropped on the talks, hoping to gain more information about her father's opinions and to shape her own.

Madeleine's single-minded focus impressed her peers so much that the entry under her senior yearbook photo says, "Her constant interest in anything she is doing, and the drive with which she does it, keep all interested in the activities of our . . . companion."

By the time Madeleine graduated from high school in 1955, she had lost her British accent. But English wasn't the only lesson her early years had taught her. "As a child, living in so many foreign countries made it easier for me to adjust to different situations and to make friends—the essential skills of diplomacy." But for a young girl continually starting life over in different parts of the world, diplomacy can simply mean being accepted, and Mandula Korbel supplied that model. "My mother always taught me to be open and friendly with new people," Albright recalled. "She said I could learn a lot from them, and she was right."

*Madeleine Albright with her twin daughters Alice and Ann in 1961*

# Chapter FIVE

# Dr. Mom

**In the fall of 1955, Madeleine left the com**fort and security of her parents' home to attend Wellesley College in Massachusetts on scholarship. She had become an expert at blending into American culture. Just like the other women on campus, she wore the popular clothing styles of the 1950s—bermuda shorts, shetland sweaters, and camel-hair coats. But she left off one popular accessory—the "I Like Ike" campaign button, which indicated support for Republican presidential candidate Dwight D. Eisenhower in the 1956 election. For Madeleine, this was more than a fashion statement; it was a political one. She refused to trade on her beliefs just to fit in.

President Eisenhower, a popular World War II hero,

*Governor Adlai Stevenson of Illinois, Democratic candidate for president in 1952 and 1956*

was the favorite candidate at Wellesley. He had beaten his opponent, Adlai Stevenson, in the presidential election four years earlier. By 1956, he had a new weapon in his campaign arsenal—television. Since the 1952 election, the number of American homes with TV sets had doubled, which meant two-thirds of all U.S. households had one. Although Eisenhower had suffered a heart attack and had undergone surgery since the 1952 election, he was able to use television to deliver an important presidential speech to the American people just a few days before they went to the polls. Voters gave Ike an even bigger victory in 1956 than they had given him in 1952.

*President Dwight D. Eisenhower at his desk*

Although Madeleine was not yet an American citizen, she had campaigned for Stevenson, proving once again that she took politics seriously. Madeleine combined her interest in politics and journalism by writing about politics for the *Wellesley College News*. Hoping to pursue a newspaper career after graduation, Madeleine also interned at the *Denver Post* during the summer of 1957, after she'd finished her sophomore year. Two events took place during the summer that changed her life forever. She had planned for the first one—Madeleine and her family became naturalized U.S. citizens on August 14.

The second event took Madeleine by surprise. During her internship, she met Joseph Medill Patterson Albright, who came from a wealthy newspaper dynasty. Joe's grandfather, Joseph Medill Patterson, had founded New York City's *Daily News* and was coeditor and copublisher of the *Chicago Tribune*. Patterson's sister, Eleanor Medill Patterson, published the *Washington Times-Herald,* and his Aunt Alicia Patterson founded Long Island, New York's *Newsday*. Albright's mother made a name for herself in journalism by writing about crime for the *Chicago Daily News*. She even interviewed George "Baby Face" Nelson, who was an infamous killer in the 1930s. Ivan Albright, Joe's father, was a well-known painter.

When Madeleine Korbel met Joseph Albright, he was preparing for a journalism career of his own. During her last two years at Wellesley, Madeleine focused on her two loves—Joe and journalism—and continued to study and get high marks on her school work. On June 11, 1959, three days after she graduated from Wellesley with honors and a degree in political science, Madeleine Jana Korbel married Joseph Albright and became Madeleine Korbel Albright.

The newlyweds moved to Chicago so Joe could work at the Chicago *Sun-Times*. Madeleine saw this as an opportunity to work in journalism in a politically charged city. Unfortunately, the newspaper didn't see it that way. One of Joseph's editors told Madeleine, "Honey, you may want to be a reporter, but you can't be on a competing paper, and you can't be on the paper that your husband works on, so why don't you find another career?" Although she was angry,

Madeleine didn't fight the system. She said, "It was 1960 and I was happily married to the man of my dreams." Even though her mother-in-law had defied her powerful father by pursuing a career as a reporter at a newspaper that competed with his, Madeleine took the editor's advice and decided to drop out of journalism. Instead of working as a reporter, she worked in a public relations office for a short time that year.

She could not have planned the route her life would take the following year. In 1961, the Albrights moved to Long Island, New York, so Joseph could work as a reporter and executive for *Newsday,* a paper founded by his relatives.

That same year, Madeleine gave birth to the couple's first children, twin girls named Anne Korbel and Alice

*Zbigniew Brzezinski served as Albright's Ph.D. adviser.*

Patterson. The joy of the exciting event, however, was marred by the babies' bad health. The girls had been born six weeks premature, and they were very weak and ill. As Madeleine stared at her daughters, who had tubes and monitors attached to their bodies in a plastic incubator, she knew she had to do something to keep her mind off their serious condition. Able to do little for her tiny babies as they clung to life, Madeleine began studying Russian. "Once we were fine," Anne now explains, "she just continued."

Albright juggled the demands of motherhood and school. Her pursuit was interrupted only briefly by the joyous birth of the Albrights' third daughter, Katherine Medill, in 1967.

By the following year, Albright had earned a masters degree with her thesis topic, "The Soviet Diplomatic Service: Profile of an Elite," and a certificate in Russian Studies from Columbia University in New York City. When Joe accepted the position of *Newsday's* Washington bureau chief, the family moved to Washington, D.C., in 1968. Although Madeleine was deeply involved in parenting and in her own education, she continued to pursue her interest in politics and foreign policy through her studies. The move to Washington meant she'd now be right at the center of both.

Albright, however, focused on the path she'd already begun—pursuing her Ph.D., which meant waking up at 4:30 A.M. every day. She also volunteered on the board of directors of the twins' private school. As a board member, she often headed fundraising activities. With the help of housekeepers, she maintained the household and squeezed in her hobby of knitting while she sat in movie theaters with her daughters. While the children enjoyed horseback riding or dance and music lessons, Madeleine bought the groceries. Although these grueling hours and long days enabled her time for both family and academics, the two were not mutually exclusive. As the four Albright females worked on their homework together, Madeleine reminded them, "There's no such thing as luck. What you get you work for."

Zbigniew Brzezinski, the head of Columbia's Institute on Communist Affairs, served as Albright's Ph.D. adviser, guiding her through her doctoral thesis. Albright's intelligence and love of foreign policy made her his star student. Her dissertation topic, "The Role of the Press in Political Change: Czechoslovakia 1968," combined her interest in journalism and politics in her homeland.

Although she still hadn't been employed, Albright saw motherhood, education, and volunteerism as part of the much larger experience women typically gained on the way to paid labor. "Women's careers don't go in straight lines. They zigzag all over the place," she has said. As if to prove her theory, her fundraising experience at her children's school led her indirectly into politics.

*Albright worked on the 1972 presidential campaign of Senator Edmund Muskie of Maine.*

# Chapter SIX

# Politics As Usual

**Senator Edmund Muskie of Maine campaigned** for the Democratic Party's nomination to run for president of the United States in 1972. Albright had done such a good job fundraising for her daughters' school, she decided to put those skills to work on Muskie's campaign. She heeded the call and met the man who became her political mentor.

Muskie found his new volunteer just in time. Money was running out. Even though Albright worked for the campaign as a volunteer, she was an enthusiastic and effective worker. In addition to using her knowledge about fundraising, she used her husband's list of publishing contacts. Many of Joe's wealthy colleagues and friends quickly donated large sums of money. As the new funds revitalized his campaign, the presidential candidate had to take notice of his star worker. Muskie welcomed Albright personally as well as politically. She became close friends with the candidate and his wife, Jane.

The senator lost the nomination to George McGovern, who went on to lose to Republican incumbent Richard Nixon in the general election. Muskie returned to the Senate and Albright continued work on her Ph.D. By 1975, however, Muskie began campaigning again—this time for his Maine Senate seat. He knew exactly whom to call. With Albright's help, the incumbent senator easily defeated his Republican opponent.

Although Albright had acted primarily as a fundraiser during the campaign, her knowledge of international relations had impressed Muskie, a member of the Senate's foreign relations committee. In 1976, the senator asked Albright to join his staff as chief legislative assistant. At 39 years old, Albright began her first long-term, paying job. Because she'd just earned her Ph.D. that year, Albright explained, Senator Muskie could introduce her "as Dr. Albright, instead of Madeleine Albright, little housewife."

Full-time work meant changes in the Albright household, but the girls never felt short-changed, and Madeleine instructed them to call her at work whenever they needed her. In her new position, Albright worked closely with Senator Muskie and frequently accompanied him onto the Senate floor for votes and

*In 1978, President Jimmy Carter,* center, *met with President Anwar el-Sadat of Egypt,* left, *and Prime Minister Menachem Begin of Israel,* right, *to work out a major agreement between the two countries.*

debates. Anne, Alice, and Katie didn't really understand what their mother did at work, which led to some comical moments. One day the girls called their mother, and the receptionist explained that Madeleine couldn't take calls because she was on the floor with the senator. "What were you doing on the floor with Senator Muskie?" they asked when their mother called back. Albright explained that she and the senator were standing on the floor of the Senate chamber in the Capitol, not sitting on the office floor.

On July 18, 1977, Albright's father, who had been the most influential person in her life, died of cancer. She took comfort in the knowledge that his legacy as a respected foreign policy expert still lived in his numerous writings and in her continuing interest in foreign policy and international relations.

That same year, President Jimmy Carter appointed Zbigniew Brzezinski to head the National Security Council, the highest defense planning group in the government. In 1978, Brzezinski, Albright's former adviser, asked her to work with him as a congressional liaison. She served as a go-between for Congress and the National Security Council. For the next three years, she used the skills and contacts she'd gained in the Senate to assist in her new position. She left the position when former California governor Ronald Reagan defeated Carter in the 1980 presidential election and brought his own staff to the White House.

Albright was not defeated, however. In 1981, she won an international competition for a fellowship at the Woodrow Wilson International Center for Scholars at the Smithsonian Institution in Washington, D. C., by writing a manuscript titled "Poland, The Role of the Press in Political Change."

Albright had won awards, worked in the White House, made impressive contacts, and raised three children. She seemed to have everything she'd wanted. Her hard work had paid off, and she was climbing up the ladder of success. Then suddenly, a major event knocked her down several rungs. "This marriage is dead," her husband, Joe, told her in 1982. "I'm in love with somebody else."

The unexpected announcement devastated Albright. Her happy family had not been as happy as she had believed. Shocked and angered by the breakup, she moped and complained about it for a long time. Finally, friends convinced her to get over Joe and get on with her life. Albright said, "I think if it [the divorce] taught me anything, it was to rely on my own judgment and to do what I needed to do for my daughters and for myself."

After the divorce, she remained in the family home in Washington, D. C., and also kept a farm the family owned in Virginia. Decorated with a cow theme, the farmhouse, on 370 acres of land, was a place where the private Madeleine Albright could escape to sink her bare feet into the dirt of her garden, see a movie in a nearby town, or knit. She could break free of the professional obligations usually demanded of her.

*Albright with her daughters Alice, Anne, and Katie,* from left to right

*Georgetown University viewed from across the Potomac River*

Albright began to teach at the School of Foreign Service at Georgetown University in Washington, D. C., where she remained for 11 years. When the sun was shining, Albright walked three blocks to work, but when the weather wasn't so pleasant, she welcomed the opportunity to cruise to school in her sporty, copper and black Datsun 280ZX. She was thrilled to be back in the classroom, and she welcomed the opportunity to give long lectures and to question guest speakers. She showed her enthusiasm by cheering at Georgetown home basketball games.

As head of the Women in Foreign Service Program, Albright felt she had a special responsibility to prepare her female students for the demands in a field dominated by men. She hosted brown-bag lunches for the women in the program and shared her own success story with them. She told them to speak out. "I basically taught people never to raise their hands and [to] interrupt," she says, explaining that otherwise other people will take credit for their good ideas. "And I think that's what women need to do." And that's what she let them—and her male students—do in her classroom. Georgetown University alumni Alex Gershanik took Albright's US-USSR Relations course during the 1989-1990 school year. The class had only about a dozen students. Albright encouraged lively discussion and interrupted only to moderate, clarify points, or provide information.

At the time the class took place, the USSR—also called the Soviet Union of Socialist Republics—was undergoing great, minute-to-minute political changes. A democratic form of government was replacing Communism, and the states that made up the Soviet Union were becoming separate countries. Albright diligently prepared for each class session—reading, watching, and listening to each day's news report to learn the latest information regarding the Soviet Union's transition from Communism to democracy. She occasionally spoke to the class about her experiences living in Central Europe and coming to the United States. "She was very big into freedom and independence, so she seemed to have a strong passion for democratic values," Gershanik explained." Because she had lived in many different countries and had known tyranny and democracy personally, she brought a world view into the classroom that many other professors weren't able to know.

Albright's classes were distinct in other ways, too. Her style was different from other teachers. "More than almost any professor, she valued our opinions," Gershanik recalled. "She was always reasonable about things—even though she was obviously strong in her principles."

Albright also made role-play a crucial part of her classes. She asked students to assume the parts of government officials, and she required women to act the roles of men. Although Albright was a tough professor who refused to grant extensions on incomplete course work, her students rewarded her untraditional teaching style by voting her favorite teacher in the School of Foreign Service four times.

Albright returned the favor to her classes. At the end of the semester, she invited all the students in Gershanik's class to her Georgetown home for dinner. "Professors at colleges generally have a social class orientation, where they hang out with professors, and students hang out with students. That's not the way she was," Gershanik said. As the students dined and discussed foreign policy with their teacher, they quickly forgot where they were and whom they were with. Albright put them at ease with her familiar, friendly style, treating them as equals and as honored guests. Even after the students had graduated from Georgetown, she sometimes took the time to send

*Albright served as foreign policy coordinator for Democratic presidential candidate Walter Mondale in 1984.*

some of her favorite pupils a Christmas card with a personal, handwritten note.

There is some dispute regarding just how popular Professor Albright was with many of the other faculty members at the university, however. Most sources say that her colleagues believed she was qualified to teach only undergraduates, so the university allowed her to teach only one graduate level course about women in foreign affairs. But in his biography of Albright, Thomas Blood said that it was the School of Government that snubbed her because she had not worked her way through graduate school there. He said that she did teach other graduate courses.

At this same time, Professor Albright began hosting salons—evening gatherings in her Georgetown home where politicians and foreign policy experts whom she had met through campaign work and the university came to discuss international relations. "They are working dinners where people can surface their ideas to see what their validity is," the host explained. "People don't feel it is a confrontational setting; they feel it is a comfortable setting." Richard Moe, a political activist who attended many of Albright's salons, once described the evenings this way:

> She thinks about it [a discussion topic] ahead of time and usually starts with a five-minute scene setter. She asks questions and tries to get people to respond. It's not hard because these are people who have ideas and want to talk about them. She will try to lead the discussion in a direction. If it lends itself to a conclusion, fine. Sometimes it does and sometimes it doesn't.

Duplicating the atmosphere that made her childhood home so exciting, Albright made many important contacts through her salons. Washington's political elite came to know not only Albright's name but also her ideas. The guest list included mostly prominent Democrats, such as Bill Clinton, who was then governor of Arkansas. Eventually, dinner guests included foreign dignitaries and heads of state, such as Great

Britain's prime minister Margaret Thatcher.

Albright also continued to work on political campaigns. She served as the foreign policy coordinator for Democratic presidential candidate Walter Mondale and his vice presidential running mate, Geraldine Ferraro—the first woman to run for executive office on a major party ticket. Albright had the opportunity not only to tell women to make their own way in the government but also to help a woman do that. Once again her various professional and educational skills

*Walter Mondale with vice presidential candidate Geraldine Ferraro, the first woman to run for that office*

*Albright was senior foreign policy adviser for Democratic presidential candidate Michael Dukakis in 1988.*

came together to make her especially qualified for her responsibilities in the 1984 election. "She was the perfect teacher," Ferraro said.

The vice presidential candidate was a willing student and relied heavily on Albright's knowledge. And as much as she respected Albright, she also liked her personally. "We hit it off right away," Ferraro said. "We tape-recorded our conversations, and I used to take the tapes with me and listen to them in the bathtub."

Mondale and Ferraro lost the election to President Ronald Reagan and Vice President George Bush. Albright volunteered again during the 1988 presidential campaign when Governor Michael Dukakis of

Massachusetts ran against George Bush for the presidency. Albright welcomed the chance to prepare candidates for the tough issues they faced on the campaign trail. "The idea that I would be able to help somebody become president of the United States by working in an area I like was perfect," she said. She decided to hire a secretary to help her handle the extra workload.

As senior foreign policy adviser to candidate Dukakis, Albright used her connections to provide the candidate with a variety of opinions from which he could formulate his own positions. Each morning Dukakis called her to discuss the morning's news. She wrote some of his speeches, and most of the people who wanted to discuss foreign policy matters with the candidate had to go through Albright first.

By this time, she had developed a reputation in some foreign policy circles of being a good organizer but not a thinker—someone with ideas. "Madeleine is not an ideologue," a former colleague at the National Security Council explained. "She's an implementer." According to critics, Albright could carry out the ideas of other people, but she didn't have any ideas herself.

However, Dukakis campaign manager Susan Estrich said that Albright did have her own ideas and was capable of much more than explaining those of other people. Remembering a July 3, 1988, incident when a U.S. Naval ship accidentally shot down an Iranian civilian plane, killing all 290 passengers, she said

*Madeleine Albright on the Dukakis campaign trail in 1988*

there was no time to gather the opinions of other people. Albright responded quickly to the crisis by helping Dukakis prepare his public statement. "It was a day for good judgment," Estrich said, and according to her, that's exactly what Albright possessed.

"I think there is a tendency to write about the fact that women entertain and men hold meetings," Albright reminded people during the campaign. "I think that is a mistake. I am a woman who has had a lot of opportunities. I've worked hard to get my credentials together and I have the feeling I am able at this stage to make a contribution."

*President Bill Clinton chose Madeleine Albright to be the U.S. ambassador to the United Nations.*

## *Chapter* **SEVEN**

# TROUBLE AND TRIUMPH

**THE CENTER FOR NATIONAL POLICY IS A NONPROFIT,** nonpartisan group that studies major political and governmental issues. The organization's members include people in government, business, and education. In 1989, Albright's close friend, Senator Edmund Muskie, asked her to serve as president of the organization. She agreed and began her three-year tenure in the position.

That same year, two other significant events occurred. Albright's mother, Mandula Korbel, died, and Czechoslovakia, her native country, underwent a major political upheaval. In November 1989, several thousand opponents of the Communist regime held demonstrations to force the Communists to give dem-

*When President Vaclav Havel of Czechoslovakia visited the United States in 1990, Albright served as his interpreter.*

ocratic control back to the country's citizens. Opposition leader Vaclav Havel became the new president, and in June 1990, free elections were held. When Havel made a state visit to the United States later that year, Albright served as his escort, interpreter, and adviser. When he first arrived in Washington, Albright hurried over to the Czech embassy to tell him about the politicians he would be meeting during his visit. Havel liked Albright so much that he asked her to accompany him on his trip to New York City, and she agreed.

Havel, who was a poet as well as a politician, was a guest of honor at a party hosted by the *New York Review of Books*. Albright was his constant companion for the evening since he kept insisting, "Stay here; you've got to do translating for me." Although Albright was used to translating, this was no ordinary audience. Havel was discussing literature with some of the country's greatest contemporary writers—playwrights Arthur Miller and Edward Albee and novelists William Styron and Norman Mailer.

In May 1990, Havel invited Albright to stay in his castle in Prague, Czechoslovakia, and in August of that year, she joined him, his wife, and his foreign policy adviser for a Bermuda vacation. She describes the island trip as "the most stunning two days of my life." The group discussed topics as diverse as the stars in the sky—Havel's writings, Albright's political passions, and the political situation in Eastern Europe and Russia.

The new political openness in Czechoslovakia provided another change in Albright's life. The amount of mail she received increased dramatically. Czech correspondents sought her help in getting to the United States and in getting medical care to their country. As she read the contents of some of these letters, however, she began to gain information about her family. She learned that some or all of her family was of Jewish origin. Albright, who had been a baptized Catholic and later became an Episcopalian, wasn't sure what to think about the letters. "Some were vague and didn't jibe at all," she said. "Very rarely did I get a letter where all the facts made sense." Since she was certain some of the information about her parents was inaccurate, she didn't know how much she could believe. She put the letters aside and focused on her family and career.

Because of Albright's position as the president of the nonpartisan Center for National Policy, she couldn't participate directly in the 1992 presidential campaign, but she served in an informal, advisory role. Together with other foreign policy experts, she worked on position papers for the Democratic nominee, Governor Bill Clinton of Arkansas.

After Clinton won the November election, Albright received a call from a member of the president-elect's staff. The staff member asked if she was interested in becoming the United States representative to the United Nations, a position more commonly referred to as UN ambassador. When Albright expressed her interest, the staff member told her to fly to Arkansas immediately to meet secretly with the future president. Albright faced one problem, however. "It was a little sticky, because I was hosting a party the next evening," she said. Albright called her guests to cancel the event—but she wasn't allowed to tell them why. The would-be partygoers soon learned why they had been "uninvited." With her daughters by her side in Little Rock, Arkansas, Albright listened as Clinton announced that she was his selection for UN ambassador.

After the Senate unanimously confirmed the nomination on February 6, 1993, she became Ambassador

*A view of the United Nations headquarters in New York City*

Albright, following in her father's footsteps. President Clinton made the UN ambassadorship a cabinet position, which meant that she would participate in top-level meetings with the secretaries of state, education, and defense and other department heads. As ambassador, she also became a member of the National Security Council, which included the joint chiefs of staff, the secretary of defense, and the national security adviser. With other council members, Albright consulted with the president on national security and foreign policy matters. She took her job very seriously. "I see more foreigners per day than anyone else in the administration," she explained. "I'm on the front lines of foreign policy every day, interpreting how people are relating to our foreign policy."

Getting the information from UN foreign representatives to the Clinton administration often meant flying between New York City and Washington, D. C., five times a week. To make the schedule tolerable, Albright had two homes—her home in Washington and the UN ambassador's official residence at the Waldorf-Astoria Hotel in New York, where American artwork and photos of her family hung on the walls. When she wasn't attending meetings, she was talking on the telephone, getting the latest updates from her assistants. "I do have a bit of 'telephone-itis,'" she once joked when someone brought this to her attention.

*As UN ambassador, Albright had to commute between New York and Washington, D. C., frequently.*

*In her official residence in the Waldorf-Astoria, Ambassador Albright frequently entertained important guests.*

It's no wonder why. As the UN spokesperson on foreign policy for the United States, Albright had to prepare carefully. Her supporters say that in addition to explaining U.S. policy, she helped shape it. In order to hear the other side of an argument, gain information, or get her point across, Albright hosted several breakfasts, lunches, and dinners each week. Sometimes the guests were members of her staff whom she wanted to get to know better. Sometimes they were presidential appointees or members of Congress whom she wanted to introduce to other government officials. Albright even hosted a dinner for singer Barbra Streisand, a close friend who often supports Democratic politicians and causes.

*Ambassador Albright meets with a sixth grade class from Louisiana to return Geo Bear. The teddy bear traveled with her and with Vice President Gore as part of a social studies class.*

Albright wanted to push international issues beyond Washington circles and bring them to the attention of the general public. She wanted to make everyone understand why she believed the UN must continue to exist. Part of her belief was based on her firsthand experience as a child seeking safety in foreign countries. "All of us are affected by problems around the world," she explained. "Many refugees come to the United States and will end up in communities across the country. But if you have an organization that promotes people talking to each other to work out conflicts, they may be able to live peacefully and in good health in the country where they were born." She believed that the United Nations was most helpful to children because the organization worked toward creating a better world for them as adults. She liked to imagine that in the future all people would live without war, hunger, or disease.

Albright made frequent television appearances to communicate the importance of the United Nations to people. Her busy lifestyle meant she had very little time for herself, but she believed that "it's important to use whatever time one has to talk to the public, because in a democracy you have to have public support for policy." When people told her that she came across well on television, Albright credited her success to her

*Albright explains U.S. policy on the* Today *show.*

*In 1993, UN ambassadors vote on a resolution to send more troops to Bosnia and Herzegovina.*

experience speaking in front of a classroom at Georgetown University for 11 years.

Not everyone applauded Albright's efforts, however. Critics said that her media appearances demeaned the office and the importance of foreign policy. Some dubbed her "Ambassador Halfbright." They believed that people who learned about foreign policy by watching television weren't as serious about the subject as those who studied books or read news magazines and newspapers.

Her no-nonsense style also drew some criticism. Rather than getting information or advice on a foreign country by taking the traditional route through assistants, she often bypassed lower personnel on the chain of command and went to those who were higher up. Albright often skipped the banquets and parties that other UN members attended. Many called her harsh and abrupt since she practiced her belief that "it's important to say what you think." She wasted no time in meetings, quickly getting to the point and asking others to do the same. In one UN speech criticizing Cuba for shooting down a small plane flown by protesters in international airspace, Albright used a Spanish word that many of her colleagues considered vulgar and inappropriate for the setting. "She can be biting," one critic explained of her style toward opponents.

As a teenager, Albright had had a reputation for being extremely serious, but as an adult she often exhibits her sense of humor. Albright, who was the only woman on the 15-member UN Security Council (the main peace-making and peace-keeping body at the United Nations), often joked about wearing the only skirt among all the suits. On Valentine's Day, she gave each of her male colleagues a red bag of cookies decorated with hearts. Unfortunately, some council members didn't know how to react since they weren't familiar with the holiday. Albright also danced the Macarena for the group in 1996, when that dance craze became popular in the United States.

While at the UN, Albright dealt with many international problems. After years of observing shockingly evil war crimes and an exceedingly high death count

*Bosnian defenders of the city of Srebernica, which has fallen to Serb forces, carry their wounded comrades to safety.*

during the civil war in Bosnia and Herzegovina, Albright pressed for U.S. involvement. Colin Powell, who was chairman of the Joint Chiefs of Staff, argued against U.S. military involvement in the conflict. Albright asked Powell, "What's the point in having this superb military you're always talking about if we can't use it?" In his biography, Powell says that he was shocked by Albright's casual attitude regarding U.S. troops. "American GIs were not toy soldiers," he thought, then explained to her his belief that the United States would be successful only if they came up with clear goals.

*Ambassador Albright in Bosnia and Herzegovina.*

After listening to President Clinton's other foreign policy advisers debate the issue at a March 1995 meeting, she interrupted, telling the men, "It's nice to think about all these things we hope to do or wish we could do, but you better start figuring out what we're going to do and whether we're going to send in troops to enforce a cease-fire." U.S. troops entered the region later that year.

And when she held firm on her position to see that the brutal leaders of the war in the former Yugoslavia were punished for their crimes, one of the leaders named a goat after her. A supporter of her position sent her a pin to add to her brooch collection—a goat head.

In fact, even though Albright prided herself in being outspoken, sometimes she let her pins do the talking. When she was in a good mood, the ambassador often wore a balloon. A bumblebee indicated that she was ready to "float like a butterfly, sting like a bee," former heavyweight boxing champion Muhammad Ali's motto. Her snake pin was a gift that she received when the Iraqi press began calling her a serpent. She wore it instead of a name tag when she met with an Iraqi official.

*Albright, wearing her balloon pin, testifies during a Senate Foreign Relations Committee hearing on Capitol Hill.*

*Albright,* above, *addresses the Security Council about pressuring the military leaders in Haiti to allow a UN mission to land and to accept the return of elected president Jean-Bertrand Aristide.*

Albright proved her devotion to democracy when the United States sought UN approval for an American military presence in Haiti, a country in the West Indies. On September 30, 1991, a military coup had ousted Jean-Bertrand Aristide, Haiti's first democratically elected president. From UN headquarters in 1994, Albright told the leaders of the coup, "You can leave voluntarily and now, or you can leave involuntarily and now." Because of her diplomatic negotiations, the UN Security Council granted approval for U.S. intervention. By October, Aristide was back in office.

*On October 15, 1994, Aristide arrives at the airport in Port-au-Prince, Haiti, and waves to cheering citizens.*

Albright was a devoted ambassador to the United Nations, and her life was filled with negotiations, speeches, meetings, and trips. She explained, "The United States has been so incredibly generous to my family that I feel it is the right thing to do whatever I can for American interests at the UN, and to make the United Nations more useful to the world."

Warren Christopher, who was secretary of state while Albright was at the United Nations, believes it is the United States that owes a great debt to her. Referring to her ability to improve functions within the United Nations and throughout the world, he said, "She followed many distinguished ambassadors, but I think it's accurate to say that none has been more successful than Madeleine has been."

*President Bill Clinton announces his choice of Madeleine Albright for the position of Secretary of State.*

# Chapter EIGHT

# MADAM SECRETARY

**IN 1996, WHEN SECRETARY OF STATE WARREN** Christopher announced that he would not join President Clinton's cabinet for the administration's second term, people wondered who the president would choose to replace him. Whenever a cabinet position opens, members of Congress, special interest groups, and government and business leaders attempt to convince the president to nominate one of their preferred candidates. Each group believes that if their candidate is chosen, their interests will be best represented in foreign policy. By the end of November, Madeleine Albright's name appeared on the "short list," which meant the administration had narrowed the choice down to four people.

*Secretary of State Designate Madeleine Albright at her Senate confirmation hearings*

Albright's supporters quickly rallied behind her. Maryland senator Barbara Mikulski encouraged Hillary Clinton, the president's wife, to support Albright for the position. Hillary Clinton was an important ally since she had also graduated from Wellesley College, had special access to the president, and knew Madeleine Albright. Senator Patrick Leahy of Vermont met with Albright and asked her what she would do as secretary of state. After hearing her response, he went home and wrote in his diary, "This country would be well-served if she were the next secretary of state."

Albright waited for the final word from the president. After a sleepless night, the call finally came. On December 5, 1996, President Clinton nominated

Madeleine Albright as secretary of state, the first woman ever to be selected for the position. He told the audience at the press conference, "By virtue of her life and accomplishments, Madeleine Albright embodies the best of America. She watched her world fall apart, and ever since, she has dedicated her life to spreading to the rest of the world the freedom and tolerance her family found here in America." Although she was aware of the historic moment, Albright retained her sense of humor. When it was her turn to speak, she turned to Secretary Christopher and remarked, "I can only hope that my heels can fill your shoes."

Soon after the announcement of her appointment, Albright once again began receiving more mail suggesting that her family had been Jewish, and she became more convinced of the notion than she had been in the past. "I got a letter that was more specific in terms of the dates, and things made sense," she said. But since she began working 20-hour days in her new position, she once again pushed the information to the back of her mind.

Another matter of importance consumed Albright's time. Her place in the history books as the first female secretary of state was not yet certain. The Senate had to approve her nomination before it became official. Confirmation hearings before the Senate Foreign Relations Committee began on January 8, 1997. Alice, Anne, and Katie accompanied their mother as she awaited questioning. After North Carolina Senator Jesse Helms, the committee chairman, called the proceedings to order, another historical first occurred when Warren Christopher introduced Albright. "As far as we can tell from looking at the history books," he announced, "this is the first time an outgoing secretary of state has had the honor of introducing his nominated successor to this committee." He went on to praise her keen intellect, moral strength, and sense of history, reminding the committee that the nominee was not just any ordinary policy expert, but a woman who had lived through terrible oppression—the kind the United States wants to eliminate throughout the world. Albright's nomination was unanimously confirmed by the Senate.

Fifteen days later, Ambassador Albright became "Madam Secretary" at her swearing-in ceremony. From behind the podium in the Oval Office, President Clinton highlighted the qualities that had led him to choose Albright. "Arriving on our shores as a refugee from tyranny and oppression, she worked her way up with determination and character to attain our nation's highest diplomatic office. She knows from her life's experience that freedom has its price and democracy its rewards. Her story is the best of America's story, told with courage, compassion, and conviction."

After she took her oath of office, it was Albright's turn to describe what this momentous occasion meant to her and how her life had prepared her for it.

Wearing her eagle pin, which she considers a symbol of U.S. strength, she said, "My life reflects both the turbulence of Europe in the middle of this century and the tolerance and generosity of America throughout its existence." Albright thanked five important people in her life—her parents, Vaclav Havel, Edmund Muskie, and Thomas Jefferson, the country's first secretary of state. In her new office in the State Department, a portrait of General George Marshall hangs next to portraits of Jefferson and Muskie. Marshall was responsible for shaping the plan to rebuild Europe after the devastation of World War II.

During Albright's first days on the job, she became more aware of her historic position. When she walked down the halls of the State Department, portraits of former secretaries of state—all men—seemed to stare at her as she walked past them. The realization that her portrait will one day join theirs surprised her. "I knew early on that foreign policy was my game," she told one group, "but I never expected four decades, three daughters and two grandchildren later that I would become secretary of state. Or that I would be traveling around the world, as I was just this past week, with the president of the United States."

Soon after starting her new post, Albright received a call from her daughter Anne. *Washington Post* reporter Michael Dobbs had phoned Anne—not about her mother's travels or foreign policy or even her job. Dobbs said that evidence pointed not only to the fact that Madeleine Albright's parents were Jewish but also that her grandparents and other family members had died as a result of the Holocaust—some in concentration camps and others while waiting to be sent to the camps. (Her mother's father had died before the war.) "I was not surprised about my Jewish origin," she explained. "What I was surprised about was that my grandparents died in concentration camps." All her life, Albright had accepted her parents' simple explanation about her grandparents' deaths. She had never drawn the possible connection between their religion, their deaths, and the concentration camps. In addition to government documents, much of the information about the family's history came from Albright's cousin Dagmar, whom Albright had most recently seen when she visited Prague in the early 1990s.

The revelations drew both criticism and curiosity from the public. People wondered why Albright hadn't investigated after receiving the letters that suggested she was of Jewish heritage. After her grandparents' deaths, why hadn't the Korbels told their daughter the truth? Why had they denied their heritage by converting in the first place?

Conversion probably wouldn't have saved them from Germany's concentration camps since Josef and Mandula's birth records revealed that they were born Jews. In Hitler's eyes, that was sufficient cause for persecution. Accusations surfaced that the conversion was an attempt by Josef Korbel to climb the government ranks. Mandula Korbel told a friend, "To be a Jew is to be constantly threatened by some kind of danger."

Many people thought that Josef Korbel had the leadership ability, intelligence, and other qualifications to become the nation's prime minister, the highest elected office in the country. As a Jew, he may have feared that some people might not vote for him because of his religion. He and Mandula might have been thinking about the fact that Jews had been blamed for many of the world's problems throughout history. Or perhaps they were looking at the problems in Germany, where the Nazi Party's ideas were gaining power, and civil rights were being taken away from Jews little by little. Since her parents had died, Albright couldn't ask them for an explanation.

Albright defended her lack of interest in her grandparents by explaining that it was the result of her great interest in her parents' exciting lives. "The experience that I grew up with was communism and how

*Albright conducts her first press conference as secretary of state.*

much my father had done to combat it," she said. "My historical curiosity was primarily directed at that."

Albright may not have known about the conversion until her nomination, but the Israeli government did. Two years before she became aware of it, a drama about her life was playing out at the highest levels. George Widenfeld, who knew Korbel in London, told Gad Yaacobi, Israel's UN ambassador, that the Korbels were Jewish. After the ambassador confirmed the information by speaking with Jewish residents of Israel who had lived in Czechoslovakia at the same time the Korbels did, he passed it along to Yitzhak Rabin, the country's prime minister at the time, and to Shimon Peres, who became prime minister after Rabin's assassination. None of these men ever publicly told what they had learned, although somehow others did find out. Prior to the publication of the *Washington Post* article, an Israeli official, Colette Avital, casually mentioned Albright's Jewish heritage in a lecture delivered in Hebrew. The remark went mostly unnoticed.

Why did Albright's personal family history become such a public matter, and why would the Israeli government be concerned? Jewish law says that a person is Jewish if his or her mother is Jewish, regardless of what religion the person claims to be. If Albright was in fact Jewish, how would that affect her decisions regarding the fighting in the Middle East between nations like Palestine and Israel? The personal matter held political importance.

Albright quickly defended herself against such suspicions and criticisms and assured the public that the new knowledge about her heritage would not affect the way she conducted her business. "I always thought that the Holocaust was one of the most horrendous acts in human history," she told the nation in a radio interview. "I have always believed in the rights of people to live their lives the way they should. I have always been opposed to totalitarianism."

Helmut Sonnenfeldt, who knew Josef Korbel, said that while the family's history might hold significance, religion is not the most important factor. "The fact that he was of Jewish descent is interesting, but it doesn't make much difference in the essence of the story," he explained. "They were refugees twice." Others declared that Albright should not be blamed for her parents' actions. "She was baptized Catholic," one State Department official said in her defense. "She was raised Catholic. Her memories are of Christmas and Easter. Her parents would not say what happened to their parents. They said they died in the war."

Although Albright said that the family history never interfered with her work, she was eager to put the very private issue to rest and get back to public service. Explaining that her top priority was serving her country, she said she would deal with her relationship with Dagmar and her background in a personal way. "When I have more to say on this subject, I will."

*Secretary of State Albright meets in Paris, France, with French foreign minister Herve de Charette.*

# Chapter NINE

# Duty Calls

**Working in the State Department building in** Washington, D. C., means that Albright no longer has to shuttle between New York and Washington. In fact, her new position comes with its own plane. She also has a bulletproof vest that her bodyguards ask her to wear when she travels to dangerous parts of the world.

As secretary of state, Albright is President Clinton's chief adviser on foreign affairs and is responsible for operating the State Department and carrying out U.S. foreign policy. "Although these events may happen on the other side of the globe, they can have a real impact on us at home," she explained. She says that by working with the leaders of other countries, she's also

*Albright with Republican Senator Jesse Helms of North Carolina*

serving the interests of U.S. citizens by creating a "world better and safer for all of us."

Albright's focus on U.S. residents is the key to her policies and style. Striving to keep people informed, she continues her frequent television appearances and has a World Wide Web site. When people log on, they can find out what the secretary of state does, where she's going, and what she says. They can bring Albright into their homes, schools, and libraries to catch up on U.S. foreign policy.

On her first trip to Moscow, Russia, she hosted an international Global Learning and Observations to Benefit the Environment (GLOBE) Internet chat for half an hour, and after a few unexpected computer

*Standing in for President Bill Clinton, Albright throws the first pitch at the opening baseball game of the Baltimore Orioles.*

glitches, communicated with thousands of students and teachers from 48 different countries. Forty-four students logged on from her old preparatory school in Colorado. The students asked Albright what her goals had been when she was a student. Albright replied, "I loved Kent, but never dreamed I could be secretary of state. Kent was a girls' school. We never thought that we could be in a position to make decisions for our country. My dream was to do well, speak English well, get good grades, and start more international relations clubs."

Soon questions were coming from many countries, including the Czech Republic. Albright said, "I am honored to be the first secretary of state to host an international town-hall LIVE on the Internet." Although it was nearly 10:30 P.M. in Russia, and Albright was eager to get some sleep after her exhausting day, she heralded computer technology as yet another way to bring the people of every nation together, reminding her audience that "this will make us wiser, quicker to understand each other, and better able to work together on world problems."

Two months later, Albright threw out the first pitch at Camden Yards for the opening baseball game of the Baltimore Orioles' 1997 home season. President Clinton, who would ordinarily have pitched the first ball, had injured his foot and couldn't walk out to the pitcher's mound. Albright put on a baseball cap and eagerly stepped in for the president. The throw went only 15 feet, and Albright joked, "I think I'll stick to my day job." In Albright's mind, however, the blooper went far toward proving her philosophy that "foreign policy is not just for elites." After the president, the secretary of state is the government official most closely identified with foreign policy, and baseball is the great American pastime. By bringing baseball and foreign policy together in that one pitch, Albright demonstrated that, like baseball, foreign policy is something that everyday Americans can understand.

Albright believes that Americans must understand

how international relations affect them before they can care about the subject. Instead of taking her first trip as secretary of state to some distant nation on another continent, she stayed in the United States and visited Houston, Texas. She purchased a Stetson cowboy hat and wore it throughout the trip. Americans were used to seeing their government officials in three-piece business suits—not cowboy hats, a symbol of the rugged, American free spirit. Wearing the hat was a symbolic way for Albright to connect with average Americans.

*Albright is greeted upon her arrival in Beijing by Vice Foreign Minister Li Zhaoxing in February 1997.*

After that trip, she pledged to keep Americans informed by visiting their cities, towns, schools, and businesses and holding town meetings and other foreign policy discussions. "What I've learned is that whether you're talking to school kids or to business people, you see that you can quickly relate in terms of how foreign policy is affecting them," she explained.

Albright admits that her plan for discussion is an attempt to gain support for the government's policies, which are determined and shaped as events in other countries change. Those policies reflect U.S. views on trade with other countries, the use of military troops in foreign nations, and relationships with government throughout the world. She also believes that sort of dialogue is the strength of a democracy—a notion she

*Albright with Mexico's minister of foreign affairs, Jose Angel Gurria, in February 1997*

*Czech president Vaclav Havel decorates Secretary of State Albright with the highest Czech civilian award, the Order of the White Lion, in July 1997.*

learned at a young age. "But as secretary of state, I know we will not have that support unless we explain clearly the 'who, what, when, where,' and especially the 'whys' of the policies we conduct around the world," she says.

Although Albright wants the public to understand her policies, she also wants to hear from the people she represents. She's said, "The part of my job I love the most is working to establish a true dialogue between the people who conduct our foreign policy—that is, among others, me—and the people in whose good name that policy is conducted—that is, among others, you." She has even released her e-mail address (secretary@state.gov) to the public to make it easier for Americans to let her know how they feel about the kind of a job she's doing.

Of course the secretary of state couldn't limit her dialogue to U.S. citizens. Albright's first trip abroad was another history-making feat—something no other secretary of state had ever done. With her Stetson placed squarely on her head, in ten days she visited nine cities spread across two continents—Europe and Asia. Recalling the challenge of raising twins, she said she decided she "could do things doubly." Albright appeared to be as popular abroad as she was at home. She charmed the French by accepting kisses on the hand and cheek and speaking French during talks with government leaders. Later, she spoke several other languages at a press conference.

On March 8, 1997, Albright added another responsibility to her schedule. She agreed to be the chairperson of the president's Interagency Council on Women, which President Bill Clinton had created in August 1995. Before representatives from 189 countries met in Beijing, China, for the UN Fourth World Conference on Women in September 1995, the president formed the organization to insure that objectives to improve women's status in the world would be addressed. In addition, the Interagency Council on Women works at getting the U.S. public to understand and support these goals. The president's wife, Hillary Rodham Clinton, is the honorary chairwoman of the council, and other important government representatives are also members.

Albright doesn't feel that being a woman puts her at

*Albright presents a poster from the 1995 UN Fourth World Conference on Women to Aung San Suu Kyi of Burma.*

a disadvantage when dealing with the leaders of other countries. In fact, her daughter says it's a distinct advantage in her job. "As a working mother, she got fabulous juggling skills," she explains. "That might help her as secretary of state, but otherwise, I don't think being a woman will make any difference."

Advancing the role of women throughout the world is one of Albright's major goals. "It is being actively integrated into a foreign policy of the United States," she stated. "It is our mission." Albright believes that such a mission will be good for everyone, not just women. Because women make up more than half of the world's population, society as a whole would improve if their status improved.

Like the rest of the administration, she wants to prepare the United States for the year 2000, because ". . . as we approach the new century, we know that we cannot build the kind of future we want without the contribution of women." Albright believes that the entire world will be enriched when women's conditions improve. In her opinion, women also have something special to offer the field of foreign relations because their experiences come from juggling so many different tasks at once—home, family, education, work, and volunteerism. "Today's world needs the unique set of skills and experience that women bring to diplomacy," she urged.

Albright also believes that knowing the difference between right and wrong and acting fairly play an important part in international relations. She thinks that real democracies act justly. Because many countries in the world follow the principles the United States represents, the United States must take a leading role in defending democratic values here and in foreign lands. Sometimes insuring that people are treated well means becoming involved in politics that may not seem to affect the United States directly. Czechoslovakia and many other parts of Europe suffered under horrible governments because other nations were too afraid to stop Hitler and Stalin (a former Soviet dictator) before they gained great power. Having lived through the devastating effects of noninterference during the early advancement of Nazism and Communism, she declares, "I always believe that if you can stop something early, and you can show the support of free countries for those who were under totalitarianism, then it's worth doing." She fears that with the end of Communist dictatorships in many countries, Americans may ignore some of the other threats they face—threats such as terrorism, weapons of mass destruction, and the importation of drugs from other countries. Albright's desire to become involved overseas frightens many foreign policy experts who think that perhaps she is too willing to risk the lives of American troops to fight battles of other people in other countries.

*Chinese president Jiang Zemin shakes hands with Albright during their 1997 meeting in Beijing, China.*

*Albright attending the Senate Finance Committee hearings on China in June 1997*

In addition to keeping people in the United States safe, Albright hopes that her policy will make them prosperous. "An effective foreign policy can help create American jobs," she explains. Sometimes her goals conflict, requiring Albright to weigh a moral stance against an economic one. The conflict is especially apparent when considering trade agreements that determine how much the United States imports from and exports to foreign countries. Many people think the United States should cut off trade with certain countries until they improve their human rights policies. If the United States stops shipping products to those countries, however, that might mean eliminating U.S. jobs because fewer workers would be needed to make those items.

Trade deals with China are particularly important. Albright considers the relationship between China and the United States "the most important and significant relationship that we have to deal with as we move into the 21st century." Many Americans believe the Communist Chinese government is an extremely oppressive regime that often violates the basic human rights and freedoms of many people within its borders. Some Americans would like the United States to punish the Chinese government by setting up trade restrictions against that nation. If this happened, the United States would refuse to buy certain products from China unless the Chinese government changed its human rights policy. China would lose money, and, in turn, refuse to by U.S. products. Without the vast Chinese market, U.S. companies would not have to produce so much, and many U.S. workers would lose their jobs.

*Albright waves to a group of Israeli students after a speech in Jerusalem.*

*Dagmar Havlova,* center, *wife of Czech president Vaclav Havel,* right, *says goodbye to Albright after attending a birthday party in Georgetown. President Clinton and Hillary Rodham Clinton,* left, *also celebrated Albright's 60th birthday.*

Albright addressed this issue in an article she wrote for the *Washington Post* on June 10, 1997. She said that cracking down on China through the use of trade restrictions would lead the country "to retaliate against U.S. exports, endangering more than 170,000 high-paying American jobs."

Yet many people believe that economics cannot justify the U.S. government's trade policy toward China. These people would like the U.S. government to prove the strength of its belief in democratic principles by suspending trade relations. In response to that argument, Albright wrote, "I believe strongly that our strategic dialogue can both protect American interests and uphold our principles, provided we are honest about our differences on human rights and other issues." To many Americans, it seems strange that a woman who fled her homeland twice to avoid living under a dictatorship would not be tougher on Communist China. Reminding critics that one out of every five human beings lives in China, Albright says that cutting China off will lead us to repeat the mistakes of the past. "History teaches us the wisdom of encouraging emerging powers to become part of international arrangements for settling disputes."

Albright's openness and her frequent public appearances have made her a media darling. She told a meeting of newspaper editors, "I want you to know at the outset that I am one public official who has no complaints about the press." And why should she? During her first months in office, headlines, articles, and TV reports applauded her charming, smart, straightforward style. Her polished manner and direct answers made her the perfect TV news and talk show guest. *Time* magazine named her one of the 25 most influential Americans of 1997.

Americans seemed to agree. Albright hadn't even been in office three months when a survey showed that she was the most popular U.S. government leader. The public was more aware of her than any secretary of state in recent history. Her family's rejection of the Nazis and the Communists and its embrace of democracy struck a chord with Americans. Baseball and cowboy hats represented the American spirit. Just like the little child who wanted to please her father or the immigrant girl who needed to fit in at school, Albright cared what Americans thought of her as their secretary of state.

*Prague Jewish Museum director Leo Pavlat speaks with Albright at the gate of the Jewish cemetery before visiting Prague's Pinkas Synagogue, where she saw the names of her grandparents and other Holocaust victims on the wall.*

# Chapter TEN

# MELANCHOLY WALL

**AS THE SUN WAS BEGINNING TO SET IN PRAGUE** on July 13, 1997, Madeleine Albright stood on the steps of that city's Jewish Museum. She had visited her birthplace many times over the years, but this trip was special—not because this was her first visit since she'd become secretary of state, but because this was the first time she'd visited since learning for certain that her parents had been born Jewish.

Albright had just come from Prague's Pinkas Synagogue, which contained a wall with the names of all the Czechoslovakian Jews who had died in the Holocaust. For the first time, she saw the names of her father's parents—Arnost and Olga Korbel—engraved at eye level on the wall. Their last names were colored

From left to right, *Hillary Rodham Clinton, President Vaclav Havel of the Czech Republic, and Madeleine Albright strolling in Prague*

red. Their first names were in black. "Their image will be forever seared in my heart," she told the crowd of reporters outside the museum. (The fate of Albright's maternal grandmother is unclear. Her name, Ruzena Spieglova, was not on the wall or in town records, although other Spieglovas were listed.)

Only a year before, the secretary of state had visited the synagogue with First Lady Hillary Clinton, but she hadn't known to check for her grandparents' names. Although she hadn't asked many questions about her grandparents when she was a child, she had become very curious about her family's history since learning about its Jewish origins. Seeing the names on the wall made her think about her parents and herself as well. "As I stood looking at that melancholy wall, all the walls, I not only grieved for those members of my family whose name[s] were inscribed there, but I also thought about my parents," Albright explained as she struggled not to cry. "I thought about the choice they made. They clearly confronted the most excruciating decision a human being can face when they left members of their family behind even as they saved me from certain death."

Albright's voice shook as she read from the statement she had written herself. It was rare for a secretary of state to show such a personal side, and it was rare for anyone of her governmental rank to write a speech herself. Perhaps the most unusual aspect of the scene, however, came from the reporters who were gathered at the bottom of the steps. No one asked a single question. They just allowed her to finish, then watched her take off her glasses and walk away.

*Albright attends the 1997 Harvard University commencement ceremonies.*

# Chapter ELEVEN

# ADVICE FOR AMERICA'S FUTURE

**IN ALL HER JOURNEYS, ALBRIGHT HASN'T FORGOTTEN** the importance of foreign policy to America's youth or the importance of American youth to international relations. She knows that because children will grow to lead this country in the future, the more they learn, the better prepared they will be. Her first stop on her first trip as secretary of state was to an elementary school in Houston, Texas. Albright understands that the foreign policy she establishes as secretary of state will affect that generation.

Albright asks the younger generation to remember the history of the 20th century as they become the adults of the 21st century. "Today, the greatest danger to America is not some foreign enemy," she reminded

Harvard graduates during her 1997 graduation address. She continued:

> It is the possibility that we will fail to hear the example of that [her parents'] generation; that we will allow the momentum towards democracy to stall; take for granted the institutions and principles upon which our freedom is based; and forget what the history of this century reminds us—that problems abroad, if left unattended, will all too often come home to America.

To emphasize her message, Albright speaks on Internet chats, in newspapers, and in schools. She listens to their concerns and advice, but she also has some advice for them as they consider world issues. "No one has a greater stake in the Middle East's future than the young," Albright explained, "and it is by the young that the choice between conflict and reconciliation will ultimately be made."

Albright advises students to learn about foreign policy issues "by reading a daily newspaper or one of the weekly news magazines." Of course, it takes more than reading to improve the world. Just as she taught her daughters when they were growing up, she tells youth, "Set your sights as high as possible and pursue every opportunity." And Albright tells young people, "You will also find that the solution to every problem begins with one person taking action."

# For Further Reading

Blood, Thomas, *Madam Secretary: A Biography of Madeleine Albright,* New York: St. Martin's Press, 1997.

*Czech Republic in Pictures,* Minneapolis: Lerner Publications Company, 1995.

Haas, Gerda, *Tracking the Holocaust,* Minneapolis: Lerner Publications Company, 1995.

Holliday, Laurel, *Children of the Holocaust and World War II: Their Secret Diaries,* New York, NY: Pocket Books, 1995.

Maass, Robert, *UN Ambassador: A Behind-the-Scenes Look at Madeleine Albright's World,* New York, NY: Walker and Co., 1995.

Marx, Trish, *Echoes of World War II,* Minneapolis: Lerner Publications Company, 1994.

Stassen, Harold, *United Nations: A Working Paper for Restructuring,* Minneapolis: Lerner Publications Company, 1994.

Switzer, Ellen, *How Democracy Failed,* New York, NY: Atheneum, 1975.

# SOURCES

7–8 Madeleine Albright, "Oath of Office," Swearing-In Ceremony, Washington, DC, 23 Jan. 1997, (Cybernex Internet Service Provider, http://secretary.state.gov/www/statements/970123.html).
9 Albright, "Madam Secretary."
12 Michael Dobbs, "Out of the Past," *The Washington Post Magazine,* 9 Feb. 1997: 12, 18.
12 Robert Maass, *UN Ambassador: A Behind-the-Scenes Look at Madeleine Albright's World* (USA: Walker Publishing Company, 1995), 4.
13 Nancy Gibbs, "The Many Lives of Madeleine," *Time,* 17 Feb. 1997, (Cybernex Internet Service Provider, http://www.time.com).
13 Lally Weymouth, "'As I Find Out More, I'm Very Proud': An Exclusive Interview with Madeleine Albright," *Newsweek,* 24 Feb. 1997: 31.
17 Michael Dobbs, "Out of the Past," *The Washington Post Magazine,* 9 Feb. 1997, 13.
18 Dobbs, 13.
20 Albright, "Madam Secretary."
21 Madeleine Albright, commencement address, Harvard University, Cambridge, MA, 5 June, 1997, (Cybernex Internet Service Provider, http://secretary.state.gov/www/statements/970605.html).
23 Gibbs, "The Many Lives of Madeleine."
23 Madeleine Albright, address to the troops, demilitarized zone, Korea, 22 Feb. 1997, (Cybernex Internet Service Provider, http://secretary.state.gov/www/statements/970312.html).
24 Weymouth, 30.
24 Dobbs, 18.
29 Dobbs, 10.
29 Maass, 4.
33 Maass, 5.
34 Dobbs, 22.

35 Madeleine Albright, remarks, Colorado Women's Foundation, Denver, Colorado, 13 May 1997, (Cybernex Internet Service Provider, http://secretary.state.gov/www/statements/970513.html, 27).
37 "GLOBE Web Chat with The Honorable Madeleine Albright," Moscow, Russia, 20 Feb. 1997, (Cybernex Internet Service Provider, http://secretary.state.gov/www/schools/970220webchat.html).
37–38 Maass 6.
38 "Alumni News," *The Perspective,* Winter/Spring 1997: 19.
39 *The Perspective,* 19.
39 Albright, "Message from the Secretary of State," 4.
39 Maass, 5.
44 Madeleine Albright, "Madam Secretary."
45 Molly Sinclair, "Woman on Top of the World: The Democrats' Foreign Policy Expert's Making Her Mark on Eastern Europe," *The Washington Post,* 6 Jan. 1991: F1+ (ProQuest Access number 91337238).
46 Bill Hewitt, "Madam Secretary," *People,* 23 Dec. 1996, 46.
47 Anne Albright, "Your Mom's on the Floor with the Senator, Kids," *Newsweek,* 10 Feb. 1997: 26.
47 Gibbs, "The Many Lives of Madeleine."
50 Sinclair.
51 Anne Albright, 26.
52 Nancy Gibbs, "Voice of America," *Time,* 16 Dec. 1996 (Cybernex Internet Service Provider, http://www.time.com).
53 Madeleine Albright, "Madam Secretary."
55 Ibid.
55 Interview with Alex Gershanik.
56 Ibid.
56 Ibid.
58 Sinclair.
58 Ibid.
60 Gibbs, "The Voice of America."
60 Elaine Sciolino, "Dukasis's Foreign Policy Adviser: Madeleine Jana Korbel Albright," *New York Times,* 26 July 1988.

61 Ibid.
61 Ibid.
63 Ibid.
63 Ibid.
67 Sinclair.
67 Sinclair.
67 Weymouth, 30.
68 Maass, 7.
69 Ibid., 33.
70 Ibid., 28.
72–73 Ibid., 15.
73 Ibid., 35.
74 Kevin Fedarko, "Clinton's Blunt Instrument," *Time,* 31 Oct. 1994, 31.
75 Madeleine Albright, "Madam Secretary."
75 Hewitt, 47.
76 *Capitol Hill Blue.*
77 Gibbs, "The Many Lives of Madeleine."
80 Maass, 40.
80 Christopher, 43.
84 Gibbs, "The Many Lives of Madeleine."
85 The Associated Press, "Transcript of Clinton's Press Conference," *The New York Times,* 6 Dec. 1996 (Cybernex Internet Service Provider, http://www.nyt.com).
85 The Associated Press.
85 Weymouth, 30.
86 Christopher.
86–87 Bill Clinton and Madeleine Albright, remarks, swearing-in ceremony, Washington, DC, 23 Jan. 1997 (Cybernex Internet Service Provider, http://secretary.state.gov/www/statements/970123.html).
87 Bill Clinton and Madeleine Albright.
87–88 Madeleine Albright, remarks, Colorado Women's Foundation.
88 Weymouth, 31.
89 Dobbs, 21.
90 Weymouth, 30.
91 Madeleine Albright, interview, "The Diane Rehm Show,"

NPR, Washington, DC, 27 Mar. 1997.

91 Peter Slevin, "Like Holocaust history, Albright Story Needs Time to Emerge," *The Inquirer,* 5 Feb. 1997 (Cybernex Internet Service Provider, http://www.phillynews.com).

91 Slevin.

91 Madeleine Albright, interview, with Carol Giacomo and Patrick Worsnip, Reuters, Washington, DC, 13 Feb. 1997 (Cybernex Internet Service Provider, http://www.secretary.state.gov/www/statements/970213 a.html).

93 Madeleine Albright, "First Woman Secretary of State Madeleine Albright Talks to Kids," *The Mini Page,* 16 Mar. 1997, 1.

94 Madeleine Albright, "First Woman Secretary of State Madeleine Albright Talks to Kids," 1.

95 GLOBE chat.

96 GLOBE chat.

96 Mark Maske, "Orioles Notebook: Despite Rib, Anderson Decides to Get Cracking," *The Washington Post,* 3 Apr. 1997.

96 Madeleine Albright, interview, with *Los Angeles Times* editorial board, Washington, DC, 15 Apr. 1997 (Cybernex Internet Service Provider, http://secretary.state.gov/www/statements/970415a.html).

98 Ibid.

99 Madeleine Albright, remarks and Q&A session, American Society of Newspaper Editors.

99 Madeleine Albright, remarks, Delaware Theater Company, Wilmington, DE, 19 May 1997 (Cybernex Internet Service, http://secretary.state.gov/www/statements/970519a.html).

100 Madeleine Albright, remarks and Q&A, Kent Denver School.

101 Anne Albright, 26.

101 Madeleine Albright, remarks, special program in honor of International Women's Day, Washington, DC, 12 Mar. 1997 (Cybernex Internet Service, http://secretary.state.gov/www/statements/970312.html).

102 Ibid.
102 Madeleine Albright, "Message from the Secretary of State," 4.
103 Madeleine Albright, "Madam Secretary."
103 Madeleine Albright, remarks and Q&A session, American Society of Newspaper Editors.
105 Madeleine Albright, "Frank Talk with China," *The Washington Post,* 10 June 1997.
106 Ibid.
106 Ibid.
107 Ibid.
107 Madeleine Albright, remarks at a Q&A session, American Society of Newspaper Editors.
110 Madeleine Albright, "Remarks at the Jewish Museum," Prague, Czech Republic, 13 July 1997 (Cybernex Internet Service Provider, http://secretary.state.gov/www/statements/970713.
111 Ibid.
111 Ibid.
113–114 Madeleine Albright, commencement address, Harvard University.
114 Madeleine Albright, remarks, Seeds of Peace dinner, New York, NY, 31 Mar. 1997 (Cybernex Internet Service Provider, http://secretary.state.gov/www/statements/970331.html).
114 Madeleine Albright, "Message from the Secretary of State," 4.
114 Ibid.
114 Ibid.

# Bibliography

Albright, Anne. "Your Mom's on the Floor With the Senator, Kids: A Daughter's Story." *Newsweek,* 10 Feb, 1997: 26.

Albright, Madeleine. Address. Demilitarized Zone, Korea, 22 Feb. 1997. Cybernex Internet Service Provider, http://secretary.state.gov/www/statements/970222a.html.

Albright, Madeleine and Hillary Clinton. Remarks. International Women's Day. Washington, DC, 12 Mar. 1997. Cybernex Internet Service Provider, http://secretary.state.gov/www/statements/970312.html.

"Allright [sic] Can Be a Tough Broad." *Capitol Hill Blue.* 6 Dec. 1996. Cybernex Internet Service Provider, http://tridentgroup.com/chblue/albrightdec6.htm.

"Alumni News." *The Perspective,* Winter/Spring 1997: 19.

"As I Find Out More, I'm Very Proud." *Newsweek,* with Lally Weymouth. 24 Feb. 1997: 30-31.

Blood, Thomas. *Madam Secretary: A Biography of Madeleine Albright.* New York: St. Martin's Press, 1997.

Christopher, Warren. Remarks preceding confirmation hearings. Senate foreign relations committee. Washington, DC, 8 Jan.1997. Cybernex Internet Service Provider, http://secretary.state.gov/www/statements/970108.html.

Clinton, Bill and Madeleine Albright. Remarks. Swearing-in ceremony. Washington, DC, 23 Jan. 1997. Cybernex Internet Service Provider, http://secretary.state.gov/www/statements/

Dobbs, Michael. "Out of the Past." *The Washington Post Magazine.* 9 Feb. 1997: 8-13, 18-25.

Fedarko, Kevin. "Clinton's Blunt Instrument." *Time,* 31 Oct. 1994: 31.

"First Woman Secretary of State Madeleine Albright Talks to Kids." *The Mini Page.* 16 Mar. 1997: 1.

"Frank Talk With China." *Washington Post.* 10 June, 1997: A17.

Gibbs, Nancy. "The Many Lives of Madeleine." *Time,* 17 Feb. 1997. Cybernex Internet Service Provider, http://www.time.com.

Gibbs, Nancy. "Voice of America." *Time,* 16 Dec. 1996. Cybernex

Internet Service Provider, http://www.time.com.

"GLOBE Web Chat with the Honorable Madeleine Albright." Moscow, Russia, 20 Feb. 1997. Cybernex Internet Service Provider, http://secretary.state.gov/www/schools/970220webchat.html.

Hewitt, Bill. "Madam Secretary." *People,* 23 Dec. 1996: 46-48.

Interview. With Carol Giacomo and Patrick Worsnip. Reuters. Washington, DC, 13 Feb. 1997. Cybernex Internet Service Provider,http://secretary.state.gov/www/statements/970213a.html.

Interview. Diane Rehm Show. Natl. Public Radio. WAMU, Washington, DC. 27 Mar. 1997.

Interview. With Los Angeles Times editorial board. Washington, DC, 15 Apr. 1997. Cybernex Internet Service Provider, http://secretary.state.gov/www/statements/970415a.html.

Maass, Robert. *UN Ambassador: A Behind-the-Scenes Look at Madeleine Albright's World.* USA: Walker Publishing Company, 1995.

"Madam Secretary," *60 Minutes,* CBS-TV, Washington, DC, 9 Feb. 1997.

Maske, Mark. "Orioles Notebook: Despite Rib, Anderson Decides to Get Cracking." *Washington Post* 3 Apr. 1997, final ed.: B5.

"Message From the Secretary of State." *The Mini Page.* 16 Mar. 1997:4.

Powell, Colin. *My American Journey.* New York: Random House, Inc., 1995.

Remarks. Colorado Women's Foundation. Denver, CO, 13 May1997. Cybernex Internet Service Provider, http://secretary.state.gov/www/statements/970513.html.

Remarks. Delaware Theater Company. Wilmington, DE, 19 May 1997. Cybernex Internet Service Provider, http://secretary.state.gov/www/statements/970519.html.

Remarks. Kent Denver School. Englewood, CO, 13 May 1997.

Remarks. Seeds of Peace Dinner. New York, NY, 31 Mar. 1997. Cybernex Internet Service Provider, http://secretary.state.gov/www/statements/970331.html.

Remarks and Q&A. American Society of Newspaper Editors. Washington, DC, 10 Apr. 1997. Cybernex Internet Service Provider, http://secretary.state.gov/www/statements/970410.html.

Remarks at the Jewish Museum, Prague, Czech Republic, 13 July 1997. Cybernex Internet Service Provider, http://secretary.state.gov/www/statements/970713.

Sciolino, Elaine. "Dukakis's Foreign Policy Adviser: Madeleine Jana Korbel Albright." *New York Times,* 26 July 1988, final ed.: A16.

Sinclair, Molly. "The Democrats' Foreign Policy Expert's Making Her Mark on Eastern Europe." *Washington Post,* 6 Jan. 1991, final ed.: F1+. ProQuest Access 91337238.

Slevin, Peter. "Like Holocaust history, Albright story needs time to emerge." *The Inquirer* [Philadelphia, PA], 5 Feb. 1997. Cybernex Internet Service Provider, http://www.phillynews.com.

# INDEX

## Photo Acknowledgments

Agence France Presse/Corbis-Bettmann, 6, 76, 84, 89, 92, 95, 101; AP/WWP, 8, 9, 16, 45, 51, 59, 60, 62, 64, 66, 72, 79, 82, 94, 97, 103, 105; Archive Photos, 24; Georgetown University Public Relations, 54; Kent Denver School, 32, 36, 37, 38; Robert Maass, 2, 70, 71, 73; Reuters/Ken Cedeno/Archive Photos, 106; Reuters/Corbis-Bettmann, 80; Reuters/Sean Gallup/Archive Photos, 28; Reuters/Pavel Horejsi/Archive Photos, 108; Reuters/Petr Josek/Archive Photos, 99; Reuters/Win McNamee/Archive Photos, 78; Reuters/Scott Olson/Archive Photos, 57; Reuters/Greta Pratt/Archive Photos, 74; Richard Ellis/SYGMA, 104; F. Carter Smith/SYGMA, 98; SYGMA, 23, 48, 77, 110; Ilkka Uimonen /SYGMA, 10, 40, 53; Ira Wyman/SYGMA,112; UN Photo 152, 983/Milton Grant, 69; UPI/Corbis-Bettmann, 14, 17, 18, 19, 21, 22, 26, 42, 43.

Front cover, Reuters/Win McNamee/Archive Photos; back cover, Ilkka Uimonen/SYGMA.

# About the Author

Megan Howard has written eleven books for children and teenagers. Her work has also appeared in *Seventeen* and *Entertainment Weekly* magazines. When she's not writing, Megan enjoys gardening, reading, and cooking. She lives in New Jersey with her husband and son.